OUT IN FRONT
NUJOOD ALI
AND THE FIGHT AGAINST CHILD MARRIAGE

A CHILD BRIDE COWERS AT THE FEET
OF HER ADULT HUSBAND.

OUT IN FRONT
NUJOOD ALI
AND THE FIGHT AGAINST CHILD MARRIAGE

KATHERINE DON

MORGAN REYNOLDS
PUBLISHING

GREENSBORO, NORTH CAROLINA

To join the discussion about this title, please check out the Morgan Reynolds Readers Club on Facebook, or Like our company page to stay up to date on the latest Morgan Reynolds news!

OUT IN FRONT

NUJOOD ALI AND THE FIGHT AGAINST CHILD MARRIAGE

MALALA YOUSAFZAI AND THE GIRLS OF PAKISTAN

The world has never yet seen a truly great and virtuous nation because in the degradation of woman the very fountains of life are poisoned at their source.

Lucretia Mott
American abolitionist and women's rights activist, 1793-1880

WOMEN WITH THEIR FACES COVERED BY FULL NIQĀBS (FACIAL VEILS) PROTEST IN YEMEN AGAINST A PROPOSED LEGAL MINIMUM AGE OF MARRIAGE.

OUT IN FRONT
NUJOOD ALI AND THE FIGHT AGAINST CHILD MARRIAGE
Copyright © 2015 by Morgan Reynolds Publishing

Library of Congress Cataloging-in-Publication Data

Don, Katherine.
 Nujood Ali and the fight against child marriage / by Katherine Don.
    pages cm. -- (Out in front)
 Includes bibliographical references and index.
  ISBN 978-1-59935-466-8 -- ISBN 978-1-59935-467-5 (ebook) 1. Ali,
Nujood--Juvenile literature. 2. Child marriage--Yemen (Republic)--Juvenile
literature. 3. Child marriage--Juvenile literatue. 4. Girls--Yemen
(Republic)--Social conditions--Juvenile literature. I. Title.
 HQ784.C55D66 2015
 305.2309533--dc23
                            2014029570

Printed in the United States of America
First Edition

Book cover and interior designed by:
Ed Morgan, navyblue design studio
Greensboro, NC

CONTENTS

CHAPTER ONE:
THE BRAVE GIRL FROM YEMEN

SANA'A, YEMEN

As a child, Nujood Ali didn't really understand what marriage was. She thought it was "a big celebration most of all, with lots of presents, and chocolate, and jewelry. A new house, a new life!" Then her father signed a contract and forced her to marry Faez Ali Thamer, a motorcycle deliveryman in his thirties. Nujood Ali was nine years old.

At the time, Nujood was living with her family in a tiny apartment in the busy city of Sana'a, the capital of Yemen. Her father, Ali Mohammed Ahdal, once worked as a street-sweeper. But Aba, as he was called by his sixteen children, had recently lost his job, so there had been very little money. Nujood's mother, one of Aba's two wives, cooked the same dish every single day: rice and vegetable stew. Nujood's brothers had resorted to begging in the streets.

Nevertheless, Nujood was a playful, friendly girl with brown eyes and a shy smile. She had the life of a typical city girl in Yemen: she went window-shopping with her older sister on the weekends and enjoyed the smells of cumin, cinnamon, cloves, and sugared donuts that wafted from the city's street stalls. Her favorite subjects in school were mathematics, art, and religious Qur'an study, and she played marbles with her friends during recess.

Given the family's dire economic circumstances, Nujood's parents thought it best to arrange an early marriage for Nujood. Nujood's protective older sister, Mona, had also been married young. They had arranged her marriage when she was only thirteen. And early marriage is not uncommon in Yemen.

NUJOOD ALI (*3RD FROM LEFT*) WITH HER SIBLINGS AT HER FAMILY'S
HOME IN THE SUBURBS OF SANA'A

When Mona learned the news about Nujood's upcoming marriage, she was horrified. She confronted Aba, their father, and explained that at age nine, Nujood was much too young. But Aba insisted that when a girl marries young, it means she will never bring the family shame by having premarital sex. "Besides," Aba said, "you know we haven't enough money to feed the whole family. So this will mean one less mouth." Aba assured Mona that as part of the marriage contract, Nujood's husband had agreed to not initiate sexual relations until one year after Nujood got her first period. This is a common stipulation in Yemeni child marriage contracts.

But after Nujood was married, she was sent to live with her husband's family in a tiny rural village, and on the very first night in her new home, Nujood's husband entered their bedroom and forced her to have sex with him. This is how Nujood remembers that terrible first night:

> I'd barely opened my eyes when I felt a damp, hairy body pressing against me. Someone had blown out the lamp, leaving the room pitch dark. I shivered. It was him! I recognized him right away from that overpowering smell of cigarettes and khat. He stank! Like an animal! Without a word, he began to rub himself against me. "Please, I'm begging you, leave me alone," I gasped. I was shaking.
>
> "You are my wife! From now on, I decide everything. We must sleep in the same bed."

Nujood screamed for help and tried to run away, but her husband pushed her down and forced himself on her. The next day, Nujood realized that her mother-in-law knew about the rape and even approved of it. The women in the village believed that a husband is allowed to have sex with his wife, even if it's against her will.

From then on, Nujood suffered these rapes every night, and her husband beat her when she resisted. "With *him*, I finally understood the real meaning of the word *cruelty*," Nujood recalled.

After two months of abuse, Nujood convinced her husband to let her travel back to Sana'a to visit her family. Once back home, Nujood told her parents what was happening, but they refused to help. Her father explained that leaving one's husband brings such shame upon a family that their lives would be in danger. "If you divorce your husband, my brothers and cousins will kill me! *Sharaf*, honor, comes first. Honor! Do you understand?"

Nujood did not understand. "Honor. But this word everyone kept using, exactly what did it mean?" she wondered. "I was dumbfounded." How could "honor" mean that she must be raped and beaten by her husband?

Every year 14 million girls are married worldwide. One in nine girls in the developing world is married before her fifteenth birthday. It can be difficult to understand why parents would arrange marriages for their children, but the truth is that a girl's parents often believe that it is the best

solution for their family, especially if the family needs money. When girls get married, the husband's family often pays a "bride price" to the wife's family. In Nujood's case, her father was paid 150,000 Yemen rials, or 750 dollars. This might not seem like much, but at the time of Nujood's marriage, her family didn't even have enough money for food.

Child marriages can become especially common in countries that are extremely unstable due to civil wars or situations like refugee crises, military coups, or natural disasters.

"We are selling our daughters because we don't have enough food to feed the rest of our children!" exclaimed a mother who was mourning the upcoming marriage of her eight-year-old daughter in war-torn Afghanistan.

In Nujood's home of Yemen—an Arab country bordered by Saudi Arabia and the Arabian Sea—one of every two females get married before they turn eighteen. Nujood, forced to marry not just before she turned eighteen but before she turned *ten*, resolved that this would not be her life, that she must save herself. She would not return to her husband. She was about to embark on an incredible journey that would lead to her becoming the youngest person to ever get a divorce.

An underage, newly married couple walk together in India. Even though child marriages are illegal in India, they still take place in small poverty stricken villages. Children are married through arranged marriage by their families, but don't live together until they're older.

EARLY MARRIAGE

The United Nations (UN) defines child marriage as "a formal marriage or informal union before the age of 18," and studies show that about one-third of women throughout the developing world are married before the age of eighteen. Extremely early marriages under the age of fifteen are less common but still a major problem, with one of every nine girls worldwide marrying under fifteen. According to the United Nations, "child marriage often results in separation from family and friends and lack of freedom to participate in community activities, which can have major consequences on girls' mental and physical well-being."

Child marriage is most common in South Asia, sub-Saharan Africa, and Arab countries. The large and populous country of India accounts for 40 percent of all child marriages worldwide. In India, girls who marry before puberty continue to live with their parents until they're older. The marriages are like social contracts between the parents of a girl and boy: the families agree that their children will live as husband and wife when they grow up. When the girl gets her period, she is considered ready for sexual relations, and a second ceremony called a *gauna* marks her transfer to the groom's home.

In Pakistan, vani is an old custom where girls are forced to marry to settle blood feuds between families and tribal clans. *Vani* is still popular among rural conservative pockets within the country, although outlawed by the Pakistani government in 2005. (In some regions, vani is referred to as *swara*. In the Pashto language, spoken by many people in Afghanistan and Pakistan, the word *swara* literally describes a woman riding on the back of an animal. It is a reference to the way girls were traditionally handed over in such deals, riding on horseback or donkeys.) As recently as May of 2014, an eleven-year-old girl was married off to a man three times her age to settle a crime her uncle had committed. In the same month, a fourteen-year-old *vani* girl was recovered by police and five of her family members were arrested, including the girl's mother. In 2012, thirteen Pakistani girls, one as young as age four, were bartered to settle a blood feud.

Early marriages usually entail that the girl drops out of school and gets pregnant before her body is ready for childbirth. As a result, child marriage is associated with tragic outcomes like death in childbirth, chronic health problems, poverty, illiteracy, and domestic abuse.

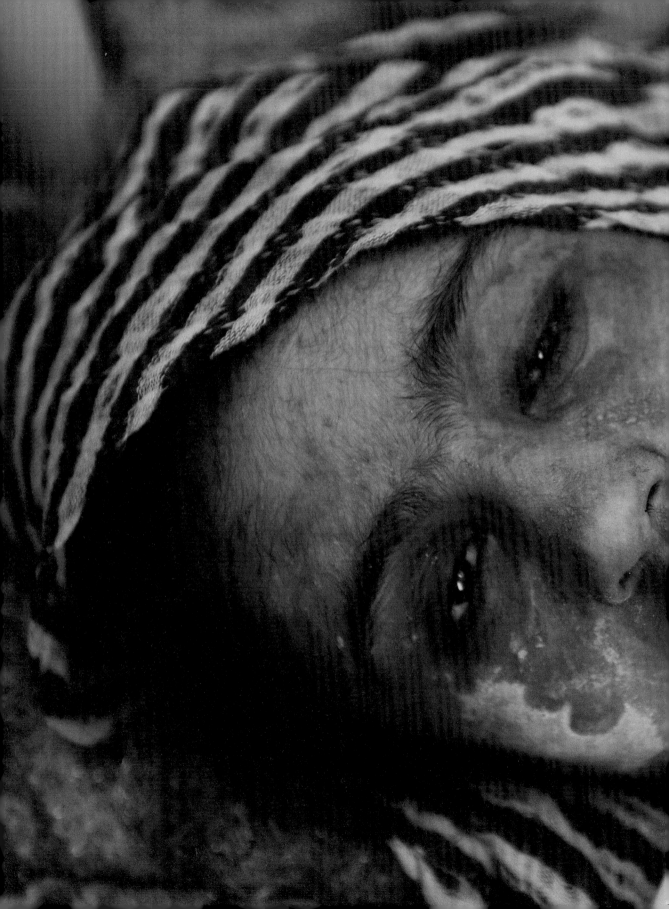

SAHAR GUL (*PICTURED*), A FIFTEEN-
YEAR-OLD AFGHAN GIRL, WAS FORCED
TO MARRY A THIRTY-YEAR-OLD MAN.
SHE WAS SUBSEQUENTLY BEATEN AND
TORTURED BY HER HUSBAND AND HIS
FAMILY. HER CASE INSPIRED OUTRAGE
THROUGHOUT AFGHANISTAN, AND
AFGHAN PRESIDENT HAMID KARZAI
CALLED FOR SWIFT JUSTICE. GUL'S
HUSBAND ESCAPED, BUT HER IN-
LAWS WERE TRIED AND CONVICTED OF
ATTEMPTED MURDER, THOUGH THEIR
CONVICTIONS WERE LATER APPEALED.
GUL CURRENTLY LIVES IN A WOMEN'S
SHELTER IN AFGHANISTAN, AND
HAS SAID SHE HOPES TO BECOME A
POLITICIAN AND PREVENT OTHER GIRLS
FROM SUFFERING AS SHE DID.

CHAPTER TWO:
THE PROBLEM WITH "HONOR"

YOUNG WOMEN IN YEMEN

It's impossible to overemphasize the role that the concept of "honor" plays in early marriages. The idea of "honor" in many Arab, southeast Asian, and northern African cultures is different than the concept here in the United States, and it's deeply connected to sex and sexuality.

In many cultures, a young woman achieves honor by remaining a virgin until marriage. A man, meanwhile, achieves honor by marrying a virgin. If a daughter has sex before marriage or outside of marriage, the shame that it brings upon her family is so extreme that she might be murdered by her own relatives. These are called "honor killings," and sometimes it's not only the woman, but also other members of her family, who are killed. This is why Nujood's father legitimately feared that if Nujood left her husband, their entire family would be in danger.

According to the United Nations, "the traditional desire to protect girls from out-of-wedlock pregnancies is a primary factor" in the prevalence of child marriages all over the world. The idea that virginity is the highest ideal for a woman has been common in many cultures throughout history, and it has terrible and violent consequences.

It seems counterintuitive, but girls are married against their will because their families are trying to protect them from dishonor by ensuring that their husband will be the only person they ever have sex with. The fear of extramarital sex is so severe that if an unmarried girl or woman is raped, in some cultures it's acceptable for the girl to be forced to marry her rapist.

This was the fate of Woineshet Zebene, an intellectual, studious girl from rural Ethiopia who was only thirteen when four men from her village kidnapped her and proceeded to rape and beat her for two days until she managed to run way. With the support of her father, Woineshet reported the rape as a crime. However, the elders in her village told Woineshet that according to custom, she must marry the rapist. After much argument with local police and judges, Woineshet and her father finally succeeded in bringing the case before a judge.

At first, the judge didn't even understand what the problem was. "He wants to marry you. Why are you refusing?" he asked Woineshet. The judge eventually sentenced the rapist to ten years in prison, but then released the rapist after he served only one month of his sentence.

In Ethiopia, there is little legal recourse for women who are raped. In fact, at the time of Woineshet's ordeal, there was a law specifically stating that a man can't be arrested or prosecuted for raping a woman whom he later marries. But when the American news media reported Woineshet's story, American women sent letters to the Ethiopian government, demanding a change in Ethiopia's marital rape law. A nonprofit group in New York called Equality Now helped organize these letters. The letters worked. In response to the outcry, the Ethiopian government changed its law.

CHILD RAPE

In countries where it's socially acceptable for young girls to marry, girls might be forced to marry men who rape them. Unfortunately, the problem of rape is not limited to child marriage. Here in the United States, boys and girls are victims of rape and other types of sexual violence. An important 2011 report from the US federal government found that 12 percent of female rape victims in the United States were assaulted when they were ten or younger, and about 50 percent of rape victims are under eighteen.

In addition to the extreme idealization of female chastity, another factor that leads to early marriages in a small number of countries— including Afghanistan, Yemen, Saudi Arabia, Senegal, Niger, and Mali—is the practice of polygamy. In countries that follow the laws of Islam, a man is allowed to marry four wives, as this is the maximum number that the Prophet Mohammed allows in the Qur'an. Each time a man takes a new wife, he might prefer a young virgin rather than a woman the man's own age. Effectively this means that for each man, there might be up to four women who are married at a young age.

UNMARRIED, VIRGIN WOMEN (*LEFT*) IN SWAZILAND GATHER FOR "UMHLANGA," OR THE REED DANCE, AN ANNUAL TRADITION IN WHICH WOMEN PERFORM A CEREMONIAL DANCE FOR THE KING. THE PURPOSE OF THE DANCE IS TO CELEBRATE THE GIRLS' CHASTITY, AND ENCOURAGE THEM TO PRESERVE THEIR VIRGINITY UNTIL MARRIAGE.

According to Islamic law, a woman's explicit consent is an important part of the marriage ceremony, similar to the "I do" vow that Americans are familiar with. However, in practice, a woman or girl does not always consent, especially if she is young. In some cases, the girl doesn't even need to be present when the *nikah*, or marriage contract, is signed. This happened to Darya, a twelve-year-old girl in Afghanistan who was sold as a wife to Haji, a forty-six-year-old drug dealer to whom Darya's father owed $10,000. The debt was repaid by "giving" Darya to Haji, who had not even met Darya when he signed the marriage contract with Darya's father.

As part of the marriage agreement, Darya was allowed to keep living with her mother until she started menstruating. In the interim, Haji would occasionally visit Darya, a spunky child with dark hair and green eyes.

"When her [Darya's] husband arrives, this carefree girl morphs into a raging, terrified child," wrote Fariba Nawa, an Afghan American journalist who wrote about Darya in *Opium Nation*, a book about the negative consequences of the opium drug trade in Afghanistan, where young girls are sometimes married to drug dealers to pay off their family's drug-dealing debts. Nawa asked Haji why he would follow through with the marriage after seeing that Darya was afraid of him.

"I do not want to force Darya to come with me, but eventually she will have to agree," he explained. "In our traditions, girls do not have the right to decide whom they marry. It's the father's right, and her father promised her to me . . . I don't want to force her, so maybe when she's fourteen, fifteen, she will know what's good for her."

In the end, Haji didn't wait long. Darya moved in with him one year later, even though she still didn't want to go.

EARLY MARRIAGE IN HISTORY

Historically, child marriage is not new—neither are births to teen parents. For most of human history, early marriage was common, encouraged, and considered normal everywhere in the world, from Ancient Rome to Imperial China. Early American law allowed marriage for boys as young as fourteen and girls as young as twelve. In the latter part of the nineteenth century and throughout the twentieth century, the age of first marriage in many Western countries, including the United States, increased dramatically. Many factors contributed to this, including changes in marriage laws that allowed women to own property, inherit wealth, and represent themselves in court without being married. For the first time, single women had economic freedom. Additionally, the availability of birth control pills beginning in the 1920s allowed some women to choose to get married and start families at a later age. Today, in the US as well as in most developed countries, individuals must be between fifteen and twenty-one years of age to marry.

But a change in laws has not necessarily led to a change in attitudes or cultural practices, particularly among conservatives and traditionalists in both the Western and Muslim world. Some in the Muslim world justify early marriage based on the belief that the Prophet Muhammed became betrothed to his youngest wife Aisha when she was six and consummated the marriage when she was nine. This belief stems from the Hadiths, stories written in the ninth century about the prophet, and not the Qur'an, which states that Aisha had reached the "age of majority." There's probably no way to know what Aisha's exact age really was when she married Muhammed, but it's clear that adulthood in seventh century Arabia is not what we consider maturity today.

Another reason that both Muslims and non-Muslims consider child marriage to be socially acceptable has to do with economic survival, as was the case involving Nujood's parents' decision to marry her off. Marriage can provide additional family support, especially in societies with struggling economies or that have recently been uprooted by political turmoil, civil war, or natural disaster. A reality of the developing world is it's very difficult to get by as a single man and even harder as a single woman.

Still, even in places like the US, there are those who do not consider marriage at a young age as a bad thing necessarily. For example, some conservative Christians have as their guide the Bible, which is filled with examples of early marriages. These parents feel the same as their conservative Muslim counterparts in that they want their daughters to marry early to avoid premarital sex and out-of-wedlock births.

An Indian marriage in 1930, in which a female child is being married to a male adult.

A TEEN BRIDE IN KYRGYZSTAN (A MOUNTAINOUS REPUBLIC IN CENTRAL ASIA) RIDES TO HER NEW HUSBAND'S CAMP. THOUGH THIS IMAGE DEPICTS A GIRL GOING TO AN ARRANGED MARRIAGE, A RELATED ISSUE IN KYRGYZSTAN IS *ALA KACHUU*, OR BRIDE KIDNAPPING. IN THIS PRACTICE, WOMEN, OFTEN IN THEIR TEENS BUT SOMETIMES IN THEIR TWENTIES, ARE KIDNAPPED. THE KIDNAPPED WOMAN IS TAKEN TO A MAN'S HOUSE, WHERE THE MAN'S FAMILY AND FRIENDS ATTEMPT TO FORCE THE KIDNAPPED WOMAN TO MARRY HIM. SHE MAY RESIST, BUT IF SHE SPENDS THE NIGHT AT THE MAN'S HOME, HER "PURITY" IS CALLED INTO QUESTION, AND SHE IS PRESSURED (OFTEN BY HER OWN FAMILY) TO AGREE TO THE MARRIAGE. IN SOME CASES, THE KIDNAPPED WOMAN IS RAPED AS WELL. THOUGH *ALA KACHUU* IS ILLEGAL, SOME EXPERTS BELIEVE THAT NEARLY HALF OF ALL MARRIAGES IN KYRGYZSTAN ARE A RESULT OF BRIDE KIDNAPPING. (STUDIES ON THE ISSUE ARE COMPLICATED, BECAUSE THE TERM "BRIDE KIDNAPPING" CAN ALSO REFER TO CONSENSUAL MARRIAGES, SUCH AS ELOPEMENTS.)

CHAPTER THREE:
EDUCATION AND THE CYCLE OF POVERTY

CHILDREN IN
THE AKHDAM
NEIGHBORHOOD OF
TAIZZ, YEMEN

Unable to escape her fate, the Afghan girl, Darya, moved in with her husband. Nujood, however, was determined to never return to hers. After returning to Sana'a and discovering that her parents wouldn't help her, Nujood visited Dowla, her father's second wife, who lived in an apartment down the street. Dowla was sympathetic and suggested that Nujood visit the courthouse in Sana'a. "Ask to see the judge—after all, he's the government's representative," Dowla said. "His job is to help victims."

The very next morning, Nujood headed for the nearest bus stop and waited in line. She was terrified. "I was the only girl waiting on her own," Nujood later recalled. "I looked down at the ground, to discourage any questions." Upon arriving at the courthouse, Nujood marched into a courtroom and spotted a man with olive skin and a white shirt. He was the judge.

"I want a divorce!" Nujood said.

The man was perplexed.

"At your age? How can you already be married?"

The judge explained that in Yemen, the legal age of marriage is fifteen. Even though this law is often broken, Nujood was the first girl to ever arrive at court for a divorce. The judge wanted to help. He introduced her to another judge, Judge Wahed, who allowed Nujood to stay the night with his family. "We'll do everything we can to protect you," Judge Wahed promised. "And we will never allow you to be sent back to your husband, never."

The Yemeni judges contacted Shada Nasser, a human rights lawyer, who took on Nujood's divorce case. Since Nujood would be the youngest divorcee in history, newspapers all over Yemen—and soon enough, all over the world— were writing about her. When Nujood accompanied Nasser to the offices of the

Yemen Times, she was shocked to see that most of the journalists were women. Nujood was beginning to realize that child marriage isn't the fate for all girls, not even all girls in Yemen.

"They have certainly studied long years at universities to earn their positions here," Nujood mused as she admired the women journalists at the *Yemen Times.* Nujood was introduced to Nadia, the newspaper's editor-and-chief, who was even allowed to bring her young daughter to work with her. "I can be a mama *and* keep working," Nadia explained.

NUJOOD, HER LAWYER SHADA NASSER, HER FATHER ALI MOHAMMED AHDAL (*RIGHT*), AND ESTRANGED HUSBAND FAEZ ALI THAMER (*LEFT*) ATTEND A HEARING IN SANA'A.

FAEZ ALI THAMER, THE MAN NINE-YEAR-OLD
NUJOOD WAS FORCED TO MARRY, AT THE
SANA'A WEST COURT, IN APRIL 2008.

Nujood was learning a complicated truth about child marriages: poorer, uneducated girls are more likely to be married young, and then once they are married, they are unlikely to receive any schooling because "wives" are expected to have babies, not get jobs. Since uneducated women are much less able to earn money for their families, early marriage creates a domino effect that traps families—and women especially—into a cycle of poverty.

"Voice and Agency," a landmark World Bank report about the connections between women's education and economic success, found that girls from poor households were twice as likely to marry before the age of eighteen than girls from richer households, and girls with no education are up to six times more likely to marry young than girls with a high school education. "Education is widely credited as the most significant factor for delaying girls' age at marriage," concluded the authors of "New Insights on Preventing Child Marriage," another recent study about the demographic influences of child marriage.

But it's not always easy to send a girl to school. Some cultures simply don't believe that girls should be educated. Even if a community supports education for girls, there might not be a school nearby. And if there *is* a school nearby, a girl's parents might feel it's not worthwhile to educate their daughter because even if she's educated, she might have difficulty finding a job in societies that discriminate against working women.

Parents of some of the victims of the 2014 Chibok kidnapping mourn their losses. Reports from the region state that several of the parents have died from symptoms related to their grief and trauma.

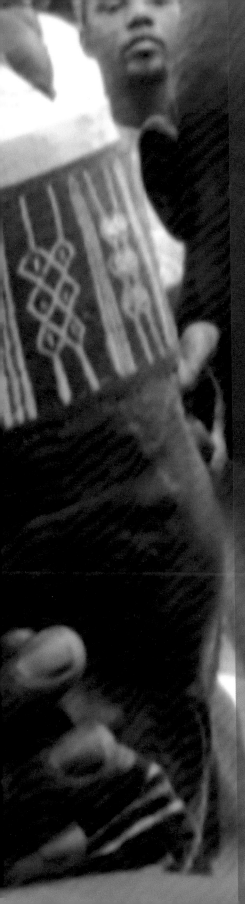

BRING BACK OUR GIRLS

In April 2014, Boko Haram, an Islamist terrorist group based in Nigeria, kidnapped more than two hundred schoolgirls during a night-time attack on their dormitory in Chibok, a village in Borno. Boko Haram's leader has threatened to marry them off or sell them as slaves. A few of the girls escaped the mass abduction, but the majority have not been brought back.

The name Boko Haram reflects its contempt for western cultural influences. In Hausa, the main language of Nigeria's Muslim north, the name roughly translates to "Western education is sinful." Not just schoolgirls have been attacked by the group. So have schoolboys, and boys have suffered a worse fate: death. The group has burned male pupils alive in their dormitories. There's been speculation that the kidnapped girls have already been impregnated by Boko Haram militants, or sold in the dusty slave markets of Nigeria's neighbors, Niger and Cameroon.

The abduction sparked demonstrations in Nigeria and around the world. Everyone from United Nations goodwill ambassador Angelina Jolie to First Lady Michelle Obama have expressed their outrage. Malala Yousafzai, the Pakistani girl who survived a shot in the head by a Taliban gunman for advocating girls' education, celebrated her seventeenth birthday in Nigeria to show her solidarity with the abducted girls.

CHAPTER FOUR:
ENSURING THE HEALTH AND SAFETY OF GIRLS

A FISTULA PATIENT IN A HOSPITAL IN NIGER. OBSTETRIC FISTULA IS A DEVASTATING CONDITION THAT AFFECTS AN ESTIMATED 50,000-100,000 WOMEN EACH YEAR. FISTULAS FREQUENTLY DEVELOP FROM COMPLICATIONS DURING CHILD BIRTH WHEN MOTHERS ARE NOT ABLE TO GET NECESSARY MEDICAL CARE.

When Mahabouba Mohammed was thirteen years old, she ran away from her home in rural Ethiopia. Her parents had recently divorced, and she had been sent to live with their aunt, who treated her terribly. But things got even worse when Mahabouba ran away to a nearby town. One of her new neighbors sent her to the house of a sixty-year-old man.

"I thought I was going to work for the man who bought me, in his house," Mahabouba recalled. "But then he raped me and beat me." Mahabouba realized that her neighbor had sold her to this man. She was to be his wife.

Soon, young Mahabouba became pregnant. When she was seven months along, she ran away from her husband and traveled back to her hometown village, but her parents had moved. The villagers shunned her, because it is considered shameful to be pregnant without a husband. Mahabouba deserved care and kindness, but instead she was ostracized. Finally, one of her uncles allowed her to live in a small shack on his property. There in the shack, Mahabouba went into labor all by herself.

Because she was so young, Mahabouba's pelvis hadn't yet grown wide enough to allow a baby's head to pass through. This is called "obstructed labor," and it's common in women under fifteen. Luckily, Mahabouba survived her painful, seven-day labor, but her baby didn't, and since Mahabouba was in labor for so long, the tissues around her pelvis rotted and lost all nerve sensation. This is a medical condition called *obstetric fistula*, which causes incontinence, difficulty walking, and painful sores. Fistulas are preventable and treatable, but since women don't receive adequate health care in many developing countries, 2 million women worldwide suffer from fistulas.

One of the problems associated with child marriage is the physical harm that results from pregnancy and childbirth at a young age. In developing nations, adolescents age fifteen to nineteen are twice as likely to die during pregnancy, or childbirth, than women twenty or older. And girls under fifteen are five times more likely to die. The problem isn't necessarily that teen pregnancy is inherently dangerous, especially for girls fifteen or older. With proper prenatal care, postpartum care, nutrition, skilled doctors, and a supportive social network, teen pregnancy can be just as safe as pregnancy at older ages. The real problem is that younger moms are less likely to have access to health care, be educated about health, or have social support from friends and family, especially in very poor communities.

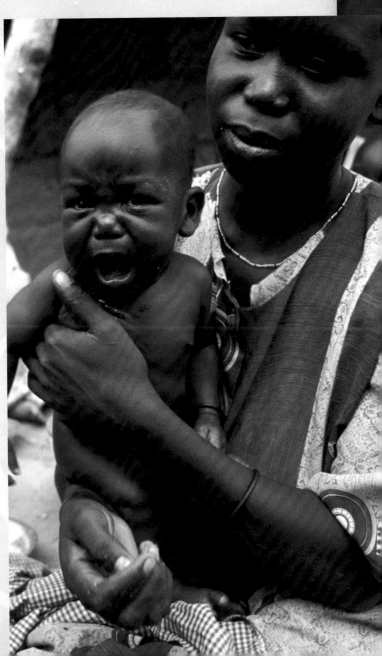

A YOUNG MOTHER IN UGANDA HOLDS HER FOUR-MONTH-OLD INFANT.

Teen Pregnancy in the US

The US has one of the highest teen pregnancy rates in the Western industrialized world. Three out of ten American girls will get pregnant at least once before age twenty. In 2013, there were 305,420 babies born to girls between the ages of fifteen and nineteen, and 89 percent of these births were to unmarried teens. According to the Centers for Disease Control, among women who become pregnant as teenagers, four out of five didn't intend to become pregnant.

Whether in the developed or developing world, statistics show that giving birth while still a teenager is correlated with disadvantages in later life. American teens who have babies are less likely to finish high school, more likely to depend on public assistance, and more likely to be poor as adults. However, teenage pregnancy itself does not necessarily cause these negative outcomes for teen moms. Rather, teen moms are much more likely to come from poorer households in the first place, and then once they have a baby, teen moms are less likely to have the opportunity to continue their education or obtain quality jobs as adults. It's therefore important to ensure that teen moms have access to social services, education, and employment, plus support from family and friends.

Education is key to preventing unwanted teen births. Researchers with the CDC found that more than 80 percent of teenage girls had not received any formal sexual education before having sex for the first time. Studies also show that teens who are enrolled in school and actively engaged in learning, including afterschool activities, are less likely than other adolescents to have or to father children. An increased availability of birth control has also helped lessen teen pregnancy rates since their all time high in 1991.

There are other health problems associated with early marriage. Child brides are more likely to be the victims of domestic violence and sexual abuse, and are more likely to contract HIV "because they often marry an older man with more sexual experience."

According to the United Nations Commission on the Elimination of Discrimination Against Women, the ability to choose a spouse with "free and full consent" and "decide the number and timing of children" is a basic human right. It's important that women and men have access to birth control and are educated about how to prevent unwanted pregnancies. The potential health consequences of early childbearing are so significant that in 2012, the United Nations Population Fund (UNFPA) deemed birth control, such as "the pill" or condoms, a "universal human right." Unfortunately, many conservative religious traditions prohibit birth control, resulting in continued unwanted pregnancies, as well as contributing to the spread of sexually transmitted diseases such as HIV.

Nujood Ali was able to escape her marriage before she was impregnated. With the help of the Yemeni judges, the lawyer Shada Nasser, and the journalists who helped spread her story, Nujood was granted a divorce. Assisted by French writer Delphine Minuoi, Nujood wrote her autobiography, *I am Nujood, Age 10 and Divorced*. Originally published in France, it has been translated into sixteen languages and sold in thirty-five countries.

Nujood's bravery and refusal to accept her fate ended up delivering a powerful blow to the status quo that allowed for children to be forced into marriages. After Nujood was granted her divorce, young girls all over Yemen heard her story, and a few sought divorces of their own. In 2009, months after

Nujood's divorce, the parliament of Yemen passed a law raising the legal age of sexual consent to seventeen.

But this is the real world, and in it not all stories end with a tidy, happy ending. The publisher of Nujood's book agreed to pay Nujood's father one thousand dollars a month until she reaches age eighteen to support her upbringing. It also bought a large house for Nujood's family in Sana'a and set up a fund paid directly to a school for her education. It is Nujood's dream to become a lawyer.

But Nujood doesn't go to school anymore. "Maybe next year," she told a visiting journalist two years after her divorce. "We had to flee during the war and ever since I didn't go back to school."

NUJOOD AT HER FAMILY'S HOME IN 2009

YEMENI PROTESTORS THROW A BOY, CLAD IN THE NATIONAL FLAG, IN THE AIR AS THEY DEMONSTRATE AGAINST THE REGIME OF PRESIDENT ALI ABDULLAH SALEH IN SANA'A ON MARCH 28, 2011.

UNREST IN YEMEN

Serious political upheaval hit Yemen in early 2011, with heavy fighting between government troops and Yemeni tribesmen. Inspired by the Arab Spring uprisings in Tunisia and Egypt, protesters rallied against the three-decades-old rule of Yemen's president, who stepped down as part of a brokered deal. A transitional government is in place. However, the anti-government uprising in 2011 gave al-Qaeda a chance to establish several strongholds in the country. Since then government forces have struggled against al-Qaeda militants, a separatist movement in the southern region of the country, and a long-running but intermittent conflict in the north. Meanwhile, the United States, a longtime ally to Yemen, has used unmanned drones against the Islamists.

In July 2008, Nujood (*right*) and another nine-year-old child bride, Arwa Abdu Muhammad Ali, cut a cake celebrating their divorces.

Nujood doesn't live in the house paid for by her book's publisher anymore either. "My father lives there. He used to beat me, I cannot live with him." Her father, she adds, "has spent all the money on getting married twice again," and she says his third wife kicked her out of the house. Nujood now lives in her older brother's cramped house. When contacted by a journalist about Nujood, the publisher conceded that it's a sad, and bad, situation. "We are unable to pay Nujood directly legally in Yemen due to the law and it is as times exceptionally difficult to know what is going on from France," said Margaux Mersie of publishers Michel Lafon.

In spite of all that has happened and continues to happen, Nujood is not bitter. She may not be wealthy, but she is free from the cruel husband who raped and beat her, free to forge her own path for good or ill. "Compared to dreams, reality can be cruel," she says. "But it can also come up with beautiful surprises."

A VERY YOUNG GIRL IS
WED TO AN ADULT MAN
IN LALIBELA, ETHIOPIA.

SOURCES

CHAPTER 1: THE BRAVE GIRL FROM YEMEN

p. 12, "A big celebration ..." Nujood Ali, *I Am Nujood, Age 10 and Divorced* (New York: Three Rivers Press, 2013), 50.

p. 14, "Besides, you know ..." Ibid., 55.

p. 14, "I'd barely opened ..." Ibid., 75-76.

p. 15, "With *him*, I ..." Ibid., 94.

p. 15, "If you divorce ..." Ibid., 96.

p. 15, "Honor. But this ..." Ibid. 97.

p. 16, "We are selling ..." Stephanie Sinclair, "Child Marriage: Documenting Sorrow," The Pulitzer Center for Crisis Reporting, June 16, 2011, http://pulitzercenter.org/articles/child-marriage-afghanistan-yemen-nepal-ethiopia-india.

p. 18, "A formal marriage ..." "Child Marriage," UNICEF Web site fact sheet, http://www.unicef.org/protection/57929_58008.html.

p. 18, "child marriage often ..." Ibid.

CHAPTER 2: THE PROBLEM WITH "HONOR"

p. 24, "the traditional desire ..." "Child Marriages Must Stop," UNICEF press release, March 7, 2001, http://www.unicef.org/newsline/01pr21.htm.

p. 26, "He wants to ..." Nicholas D. Kristof and Sheryl WuDunn, *Half the Sky: Turning Oppression Into Opportunity for Women Worldwide* (New York: Alfred A. Knopf, 2009), 65.

p. 29, "When her husband ..." Fariba Nawa, *Opium Nation: Child Brides, Drug Lords, and One Woman's Journey Through Afghanistan* (New York: HarperCollins, 2011), 104.

p. 29, "I do not want ..." Ibid.,122-123.

CHAPTER 3: EDUCATION AND THE CYCLE OF POVERTY

p. 36, "Ask to see ..." Nujood Ali, *I Am Nujood, Age 10 and Divorced*, 101.

p. 36, "I was the only ..." Ibid., 103.

p. 36, "I want a divorce ..." Ibid., 21.

p. 36, "At your age ..." Ibid.,41.

p. 36, "We'll do everything ..." Ibid., 46.

p. 37, "They have certainly ..." Ibid., 123.

p. 37, "I can be ..." Ibid., 123.

p. 39,   "Education is widely . . ." Saranga Jain and Kathleen Kurtz, "New Insights on Preventing Child Marriage: A Global Analysis of Factors and Programs," United States Agency for International Development, April 2007, http://www.icrw.org/files/publications/New-Insights-on-Preventing-Child-Marriage.pdf.

p. 41,   "Western education is . . ." Colin Freeman, "Missing Nigerian girls: Whatever Happened to #Bringbackourgirls?," *Telegraph* (UK), July 14, 2014, http://www.telegraph.co.uk/news/worldnews/africaandindianocean/nigeria/10947211/Missing-Nigerian-girls-whatever-happened-to-Bringbackourgirls.html.

CHAPTER 4: ENSURING THE HEALTH AND SAFETY OF GIRLS

p. 44,   "I thought I . . ." Kristof and WuDunn, *Half the Sky: Turning Oppression Into Opportunity for Women Worldwide*, 93.

p. 48,   "because they often . . ." "Child Marriage Facts and Figures," International Center for Research on Women (ICRW) fact sheet, http://www.icrw.org/child-marriage-facts-and-figures.

p. 48,   "free and full . . ." "Text of the Convention," The Convention of the Elimination of All Forms of Discrimination Against Women, 1979, http://www.un.org/womenwatch/daw/cedaw/.

p. 48,   "decide the number . . ." Ibid.

p. 48,   "Universal human right . . ." Amanda Beadle, "United Nations Declares Access to Contraception A 'Universal Human Right,'" *Think Progress,* November 14, 2012, http://thinkprogress.org/health/2012/11/14/1189161/un-contraception-human-right/.

p. 49,   "Maybe next year . . ." Judith Spiegel, "I Made It Possible for My Father to Buy New Wives," Radio Netherlands Worldwide, March 4, 2013, http://m.rnw.nl/english/%252Fnode/171073.

p. 53,   "My father lives . . ." Ibid.

p. 53,   "We are unable . . ." Joe Sheffer, "Yemen's Youngest Divorcee Says Father Has Squandered Cash From Her Book," *Guardian* (UK), March 12, 2013, http://www.theguardian.com/world/2013/mar/12/child-bride-father-cash-spend.

p. 53,   "Compared to dreams . . ." Ibid.

BIBLIOGRAPHY

Ali, Nujood, and Delphine Minoui. *I Am Nujood, Age 10 and Divorced*. New York: Three Rivers Press, 2010.

Beadle, Amanda. "United Nations Declares Access to Contraception A 'Universal Human Right.'" *Think Progress*, November 14, 2012. http://thinkprogress.org/health/2012/11/14/1189161/un-contraception-human-right/.

Bradley, John R. *Behind the Veil of Vice: The Business and Culture of Sex in the Middle East*. New York: Palgrave Macmillan, 2010.

Centers for Disease Control and Prevention. "Health Consequences of Child Marriage in Africa." *Emerging Infectious Diseases* 12:11 (2006). http://wwwnc.cdc.gov/eid/article/12/11/06-0510_article.

"Child Marriage." The United Nations Children's Fund (UNICEF) fact sheet. http://www.unicef.org/protection/57929_58008.html.

"Child Marriage Facts and Figures." International Center for Research on Women (ICRW) fact sheet. http://www.icrw.org/child-marriage-facts-and-figures.

"Text of the Convention." The Convention of the Elimination of All Forms of Discrimination Against Women, 1979. http://www.un.org/womenwatch/daw/cedaw/.

Chemaly, Soraya. "Fathers Are the Key to Ending Child Marriage." *Huffington Post*, October 3, 2013. http://www.huffingtonpost.com/soraya-chemaly/fathers-are-the-key-to-en_b_4036532.html.

"Child Brides Face Increased Chances of Illiteracy, Domestic Violence, Report Says." *Vancouver Sun*, May 15, 2014. http://www.vancouversun.com/life/Child+brides+face+increased+chances+illiteracy+domestic/9839453/story.html.

Couch, Robbie. "Laila Was 13 When She Was Forced Into Marriage. Now She's Speaking Up For Change." *Huffington Post*, April 3, 2014. http://www.huffingtonpost.com/2014/04/03/child-bride-marriage_n_5085081.html.

Dahl, Gordon B. "Early Teen Marriage and Future Poverty." *Demography* 47, no. 3 (August 2010): 689-718.

Das, Priya, Nitin Datta, and Priya Nanda. "Impact of Conditional Cash Transfers on Girls' Education." International Center for Research on Women, March 2014. http://www.icrw.org/files/publications/IMPACCT_Hires_FINAL_3_20.pdf.

Diehm, Jan. "1 in 9 Girls Marries Before Age 15, And Here's What Happens To Them." *Huffington Post*, December 10, 2013. http://www.huffingtonpost.com/2013/12/05/child-marriage-_n_4393254.html.

El Feki, Shereen. *Sex and the Citadel: Intimate Life in a Changing Arab World.* New York: Pantheon Books, 2013.

Fisher, Max. "'Girls are the World's Forgotten Population': Nine facts About Child Brides." *Washington Post*, August 1, 2013. http://www.washingtonpost.com/blogs/worldviews/wp/2013/08/01/girls-are-the-worlds-forgotten-population-nine-facts-about-child-brides/.

Fontanella-Khan, Amana. *Pink Sari Revolution: A Tale of Women and Power in India.* New York: W.W. Norton & Company, Inc.

Hamilton, Vivian E. "The Age of Marital Capacity: Reconsidering Civil Recognition of Adolescent Marriage." *Boston University Law Review* 92 (2012): 1817-1862.

Jain, Saranga, and Kathleen Kurtz. "New Insights on Preventing Child Marriage: A Global Analysis of Factors and Programs." United States Agency for International Development, April 2007. http://www.icrw.org/files/publications/New-Insights-on-Preventing-Child-Marriage.pdf.

Gorney, Cynthia. "Too Young to Wed: The Secret World of Child Brides." *National Geographic*, June 2011. http://ngm.nationalgeographic.com/print/2011/06/child-brides/gorney-text.

Human Rights Watch. "Q&A: Child Marriage and Violations of Girls' Rights." June 14, 2013. http://www.hrw.org/news/2013/06/14/q-child-marriage-and-violations-girls-rights.

Khan, Sonali. "Sex and Sensibility: Breaking Through India's Patriarchal Bias." *Guardian* (UK), November 6, 2013. http://www.theguardian.com/global-development-professionals-network/2013/nov/06/india-child-marriage-bihar.

BIBLIOGRAPHY CONTINUED

Kristof, Nicholas D., and Sheryl WuDunn. *Half the Sky: Turning Oppression Into Opportunity for Women Worldwide.* New York: Alfred A. Knopf, 2009.

Nawa, Fariba. *Opium Nation: Child Brides, Drug Lords, and One Woman's Journey Through Afghanistan.* New York: HarperCollins, 2011.

Power, Carla. "Nujood Ali and Shada Nasser: The Voices for Children." *Glamour*, 2008. http://www.glamour.com/inspired/women-of-the-year/2008/nujood-ali-and-shada-nasser.

Rabin, Roni C. "Nearly 1 in 5 Women in U.S. Survey Say They Have Been Sexually Assaulted." *New York Times*, December 14, 2011. http://www.nytimes.com/2011/12/15/health/nearly-1-in-5-women-in-us-survey-report-sexual-assault.html.

Sinclair, Stephanie. "Child Marriage: Documenting Sorrow." The Pulitzer Center on Crisis Reporting: June 16, 2011. http://pulitzercenter.org/articles/child-marriage-afghanistan-yemen-nepal-ethiopia-india.

"Trends in Teen Pregnancy and Childbearing." US Department of Health and Human Services, Office of Adolescent Health, July 15, 2014. http://www.hhs.gov/ash/oah/adolescent-health-topics/reproductive-health/teen-pregnancy/trends.html#.U8_ZJffD_cs.

Steinhauer, Stephanie. "White House to Press College to do More to Combat Rape." *New York Times*, April 28, 2014. http://www.nytimes.com/2014/04/29/us/tougher-battle-on-sex-assault-on-campus-urged.html.

"UNICEF: Child Marriages Must Stop." UNICEF press release, March 7, 2001. http://www.unicef.org/newsline/01pr21.htm.

"Untying the Knot: Exploring Early Marriage in Fragile States." World Vision UK, March 2013. http://www.worldvision.org/resources.nsf/main/press-reports/$file/Untying-the-Knot_report.pdf.

"Voice and Agency: Empowering Women and Girls for Shared Prosperity." World Bank Group, May 2014. http://www.worldbank.org/en/topic/gender/publication/voice-and-agency-empowering-women-and-girls-for-shared-prosperity.

WEB SITES

GirlsNotBrides.org

Girls Not Brides is a global partnership funded in part by major foundations and NGOs that are "united by a commitment to end child marriage and enable girls to fulfill their potential." The extraordinarily well-organized Web site includes searchable links to the major worldwide reports that currently exist on the topics of early and child marriage.

http://www.pbs.org/now/shows/341/facts.html

The Public Broadcasting Service's (PBS) fact sheet on child marriage features a convenient roll call of links to fact sheets from other major organizations.

http://pulitzercenter.org/projects/child-brides-child-marriage-too-young-to-wed

This is the main page for the Pulitzer Center for Crisis Reporting's *Too Young to Wed: The Secret World of Child Brides* ongoing project. Links include Cynthia Gorney's outstanding 2011 *National Geographic* article on child brides, available here: http://ngm.nationalgeographic.com/2011/06/child-brides/gorney-text. The Web site also features the photographs of Stephanie Sinclair, a photojournalist who has won many awards for her extensive work on the issue of child marriage.

INDEX

PHOTO CREDITS